To

My friends, my family,

and

Mr. D.

Introduction by the Author

So here we are. With this poetry, I have layed out my heart and my soul in every line, bound and packaged in these honest pages. What you will discover is several years worth of my musing, all of which hold some innate part of me. From a human being to the same, all I can wish for is that what humble insights I have may be shared with the readers of this book. At the end of the day, this is all I wish to accomplish.

With Great Sincerity,

Aidan L,

The author.

Static Dreams

Aidan Lopedota

Table of Contents

1. To Begin..................10
2. A Poem for Mornings..................11
3. Brief Moments..................12
4. Whitewash..................13
5. Strongest..................14
6. Close My Eyes?..................15
7. Misguidance..................16
8. Shame..................17
9. Mask of Dreams..................18
10. Figure..................19
11. Folly..................20
12. Chase..................21
13. Sent..................22
14. Conceal/Congeal..................23
15. Her Being, Held Dear..................24
16. We Went Back..................25
17. Noiseless Rebirth..................26
18. Untitled 1..................27
19. Ramble for a Reason..................28
20. Dreamings..................29
21. Untitled 2..................30
22. Remnants..................31

23. Story Book..................................32
24. I Burned Something of Mine............33
25. I Am Hope..................................34
26. Apology.....................................35
27. The Explanation of a Dream.............36
28. Finality......................................37
29. If Nature Knew You......................38
30. Ownership..................................39
31. Self... 41
32. Lost Ondine................................42
33. The Yearning Falls Away.................43
34. Dandelions.................................44
35. Summer Prayer............................45
36. Path of the Enlightened..................46
37. Released Words...........................47
38. Sleepless..................................48
39. Creature....................................49
40. Creation....................................50
41. To Retell...................................51
42. Untitled 3..................................52

1.
Untitled 1

I am the winged dreamer, the one who smiles, the determined long-runner in life:

I am a simple book whose story makes it through the rugged verses.

2.
A Poem for Mornings

Come and I will teach you
of a hero named Balance
and a devil named Truth
That fought under the whims of forgotten warriors.
I will show you that human articulateness and
human reasoning are not always the same
And that the twisted logic of Truth bears no witnesses
but the brave
Who are none but cowards and hypocrites.
The weakest who bear no shame against Sin
as long as they still seek Balance
will realize that in Balance there is no Truth that does not
firstly lie to the human heart.

3.
Brief Moments

In the moments that change the world
between death and life
life and death
waking and sleep
sunset and sunrise
and the realization of one's self.

4.
Whitewash

What does this sorrow whitewash away
Beneath the drifting shores of what is right
Grievances that I do not hold as holy
As this chipper mist broods a blundered sight

What does this wonder whitewash away
I am the force that rolls, unmoving, dreams
The undertone of what is truly felt
Undermines all ruthless, tattered seams.

5.
Strongest

My comfort only means as much as
my lies are worth on paper.
A hinge for puzzle-making
Pile for trust keeping.
I decide the sin that I own
and here do keep it;
A painted philosophy
for me to keep and me only.
I am only as strong as my conceit
only as weak as I am awake.
I am keen to digress these fears
as they are only what I believe
and as far as I'll go.

6.
Close My Eyes?

You tell me to close my eyes,
But if I close my eyes,
How will I know if you change?

7.
Misguidance

What is this thoughtfulness?
It is drowsy, it is incomplete
If you hold on, are you less likely to know?
Help me with this quiet
It has not been perturbed
Or interrupted
Such subtlety by any other knowledge would be a lie--
And a lie by any other decibel
Would be a thought.

8.
Shame

I'm sorry if I stole what you needed
God forbid you see that change is a perspective anyway
Beneath the sapling tree we've come to know as comfort
We realize that shame is just another worldly possession.

9.
Mask of Dreams

Mask of dreams
Who painted you
Who gave you wings to fly
Over my head in silent threads of
the memories you cry?

10.
Figure

This man, this wooden man
Only hold half of the screws he should
He tries to stand, he really does
But this wooden man wobbles and collapses onto his knees
This man, this unsupported man
Pity him, really do, just pity him
Not just because he cannot stand or walk
But because he lacks
Because he is incomplete.

11.
Folly

"Live if you can live, or dare if you should."
You're standing in the kitchen, begging me to stay
I reply, saying,
"In good fun or not, must you seek me so?"
But through apologies and chocolate
I have chosen to stay.

12.
Chase

When I was a child I used to squint my eyes and look at traffic lights
And utter a magic word to keep me safe
Nightmares and dreams knew where to find me
Under my soft, naive breath.

When I was a child I never knew there would be a time when I would remember
And I was not yet tainted by the world or myself
I was part of this earth, of the universe,
And if only I would have realized this
Maybe I wouldn't have to chase it the rest of my life

When I was a child I caught fireflies and caterpillars
Beneath the hazy rings of summer
I knew something more about life then
And those living creatures to me were the innate seeds of life and light and knowledge

I was everything all at once and yet small
For children are knowing yet humble
Perceptive yet innocent.

When I was a child I did not realize that I would spend my whole life chasing who I was.

13.
Sent

This is all we have,
But we are happy
This is all we know,
But we're content
This is all we see,
And it has value
We were not delivered,
But we were sent.

14.
Conceal/Congeal

You're scared,
But look,
There are two hearts out of one
But could you find the epitome
Of where you'd first begun?

Thoughts conceived
From the flesh
Of a secret thus concealed
Cry in the wanton pity of their dreaming,
now congealed.

15.
Her Being, Held Dear

I am the compassionate destroyer
Folly trembles,
My hold
Consumes

Wordless faith trespassing with
Tilted feet
Until rays of happiness beat down with an
Unnecessary consistency
Grass martyrs sway,
Mocking their own futile attempt

I am the compassionate destroyer --
And with what I reap,
I rest.

16.
We Went Back

We will die
because we were faced with a decision
and we made a choice.
We took a chance.

No.
We will live
because we saw our faults
and we knew regret
we saw the lie.

We will try
because we see the reason
because we crossed the line
and we went back.

17.

Noiseless Rebirth

My eyes burn
maybe I have stayed up too late
and done too many things
perhaps they are stained with stress
trembling honesty
sinking wearily
but tomorrow is a brand new day
with brand new words.

18.
Untitled 2

I am your protector
and I will not revoke my words
lest they be lies
this sole fact is important
as my wings are surely proof
that I can fly

Stay close under my wings
and I will not let you fall
lest there be winds
this sole notion is surely proof
that I have limits

Graze under green grass
and I will protect you from the rain
lest there be clouds
this sole sentence is simply proof
that I am honest.

19.

Ramble for a Reason

Hi--
I am your best friend
but you don't know me
so I'll go.

and I ramble for a reason
or at least I always try to think so.

there's a meter to this life and there's a secret to this lie
can you find the flow?
will you ever know?

clap if you'll applaud for me
I'm nothing but a fool, you see
the epitome of irony

so no.
I'll never show.

let's continue on our path and though
we'll always face the wrath we can
control the aftermath and what is whole.
let's set a goal.

and we ramble for a reasonor at least we always try to think so.

20.
Dreamings

Who is whole here?
Not I, not anyone
We are all tormented fragments
abysses, shadows,
twisted, broken things

Who is sane here?
not I, nor you
we all love the nights here
darkness, laughter
fragile, as hurt wings

Who is dreaming here?
Surely I, you see
we are all crazy, worthless,
beautiful things.

21.
Untitled 2

My insomnia crackles softly
Under the treads I bear to keep me safe
That churn like soldiers,
Desolate and seeking.

Threadbare sheets
So barren that I am a fool to risk the wear
They break like twigs,
rustling away.

The clock gives no solace
Times and places so apart that they are haunting
There are different eyes now,
flickering, judging.

22.
Remnants

Filthy, Filthy lies
Filter in to my disguise
I cannot hold much longer
Under the pressure of these questions

And I must think of things I've done
and hold the truth under my tongue
There's nothing more to tell you
Than revealed
The things you want to know are concealed
I'm just trying to let you know
that some things I would
rather not show
Because some thoughts need to go

So of "hms" and shrugs and "maybes"
Through frustration you must see
That I am hiding from treason
And not hiding from me

I'm not trying to shun you
But I'm trying to leave alone
If you do not want these remnants
Keep me out of your home.

23.
Story Book

Is your heart too vital for seeing
Or your mind too nervous, and set for thinking
Is the world too big for grand surprises
Or is it too small for speaking

Do you dream
If you know you have seen
The negatives of your nightmares
Do you feel
The need to kneel
Or do you grin, and fight them?

24.
I Burned Something of Mine...

I burned something of mine one day
I stood, and watched it.
Full of emotion -- I felt like crying -- or maybe that was just the smoke
Then again, it could have been both.
The pages rise and burn, turning to a pit of ash before my very eyes.
All burns but the cover, which lays decayed and charred.
The bitterly beautiful flames are so hot I feel they will ignite my whole being, my entire soul.
I let go of these words now, I release them into thought,
I banish them from existence with my own hand-- the hand that created them.
The wind blows some of the ashes toward the sky.
I am left with a cover that will not burn
My eyes sting from the heat.

I burned something of mine once
I will forever carry this line with me
In a place near to my heart,
Next to all of the forgotten things.
But I will never forget that day.

25.
I Am Hope.

Upon this shallow Death I stumble
Feet falling as I tumble
Against the Truth that evades me like
the plague.
And by our very souls we weep
Trodden Lies down at our feet
Listless pools that shimmer like
the day.
Discovery is nothing humble
I am Hope and I do grumble
This fight has worth, being only but
A Dream.

26.
Apology

If I had one day more
I would rewrite
The words that have escaped my tongue
One more day to tell you
I do not like who I have become.

27.
The Explanation of a Dream

I start a new life each day
Using the knowledge of my past lives to guide me
Through the growth of my uncertain future.
Every dawn is a new life in which I am born out of a
Subconscious self.
When I awake as this new life
I am an unchanged reincarnation
of yesterday's me.

For a dream divides two lives

28.
Finality

In the nondescript eaves of thoughts
wings that burrow down
into the great capacity of earth
dissembled pieces are broken, strangled
Evanescent words caught on fires
extinguished lullabies
a murmuring languor
Leaves that fall, unattained,
Revered in the most blazing moonlight;
Lay on the ground
in their terminal sleep.

29.
If Nature Knew You

The trees kneel humbly
aware of the lies you have dealt
and truths you've spoken
The grass in the paled sidewalk, mumbles
whispering, murmuring, gossipng
The bushes flee,
conscious of all your faults and failures
But the breeze stays
Enamoured by your beauty
and your smile.

30.
Ownership

I own this face
that gives logic a name
this is the melody
fallen to fame

truth is an eyelid
But I am quite blind
save all your alibis
force out the time

balance is a hand
fragile in virtue
your teeth chew at the wire
of all who dare doubt you

I am afraid
and I own this fear
that all that I know
is fragmented here

so deny all your nurture
find shelter and hide
escape from this sickening
human pride

pleasantries frolic
in late April air
there's a method to reason
that nature will share

we'll personify ourselves to the highest degree
and when reason is treason
you've no eyes to see
life is a pupil and love is your lashes
designed to protect all the lies that
will pass it

If I am alive
as I surely am
I will peel this uncertainty
with my own hands

and every tree
is a beautiful seed
it grows up and its soul
is stagnant but free.

31.
Self

Tiny seed of myself
I break you open on my belly
like an otter;
Little thing!
you have stayed with me.

32.
Lost Ondine

To mediate a clever disguise
Beneath the whisping, ancient tides
With winged breath, falls, floats
and follows
Through the breezes, light and shallow
And unravel between the ocean waves
Seeking Truth below the moors
To kiss it's beauty, evermore.

33.
The Yearning Falls Away

Bone breaks bone
the thing you loved and lost
shows they way
Bone breaks bone
what you love you
wish to keep.
Bone breaks bone.

34.
Dandelions

I walked
In the evening of some small town
it's cool air,
stagnant smell
the roots of weeds
push themselves
through the soil,
Between houses, gardens,
roads, lifetimes---
dandelions.

35.
Summer Prayer

Summer's eve, my soul you keep
upon sweet air and rain you creep
your night's intoxicating sweep--

Summer's eve my breath is taken
Lost forever in your salvation
O Beautiful World, can you not see
why I keep my soul in Summer's eve?

36.
Path of the Enlightened

A whisper is a conduit
that conducts the quiet earth
whose winged virtues seep through time
To give each soul it's girth

We are tiny soldiers here
who break the solid ground
To pity it for what it's worth
and leave no thought profound.

37.
Released Words

We suffer from faint amnesia
step forth,
the cracks split.
A great fissure is formed
Write down your fate,
an inefficiency
on a note
drop it down
into this crevice.

Be relieved, you have lost something.

38.
Sleepless

To those I sing
unassured that my words are soothing
I rifle through my things,
searching for something
to keep me happy
You've stayed beside me
and you don't do too much
I've set myself up
to trip through sleeplessness
with open arms
and made us both restless.

39.
True Creature

Day by day we find that these forces we extract ourselves from
Are but feeble excuses to retract the punished.

I, being but a creature and yet a servant
Am shattered false as though
My tears are a dream.

This night lingers, confused and whole,
And we mend each gash with garish steel.

It can be sure that the sin we extract our meaning from is but a
Feeble excuse
For us to fufill what we know.

40.
Creation

I wrote an altar
in the space between my rouge ambition
and my thought
I broke your shame
with the creed I carved by these hands.
I locked the door
And put the key on the other side.

41.
To Retell

Forgotten by what I know,
fallen here, with beauty
not forgotten by me;
Please draw the boundaries of this sanction
Before our compact requires I set you free
I have or have not been forsaken
Please stay with me.

42.
Untitled 3

To whatever fancies us
we may attribute the seasons;

Spring is the beginning, the intrigue;
Summer advances, it is passion,
fullness;
Autumn is contentment, settled,
searching;
Winter, desolate and ultimate,
ends this cycle.

Spring is rebirth.

www.ingramcontent.com/pod-product-compliance
Lightning Source LLC
Chambersburg PA
CBHW061515040426
42450CB00008B/1639